Joanie Boney Books

www.joanieboneybooks.com

"Aaron! Come inside time for dinner, sweetheart!"

"Coming Mom, I'm just going to grab my ball!"

8 year old Aaron Bentley had being playing Soccer in the large playground across from his suburban town house all evening. By the time his mother yelled for him through the kitchen window, the sun had begun to set behind the large oak trees.

Exhaustion had kicked in and most of his playmates had already
retreated home. Being the huge soccer fan that he was, he usually
was the last one on the field practicing his skills in his bright red jersey.

Aaron had big dreams of making his school's team. Tryouts were approaching in a few weeks and he was determined to practice until then.

Just before his mother called for him, Aaron's soccer
ball had rolled into the woods behind the playground.
His plan was to run in, grab it and head back home.

But as soon as he stepped on the brown leaves scattered all over the ground among the large trees, he heard a very loud growling and agonizing sound.

Immediately he turned his head around to find the source of the noise, but nothing. He turned his head in every direction, while his heart raced fast through his chest.

He stood frozen in his tracks, stunned and afraid to move. "Did anyone else hear that?" he asked himself.

Within seconds the howling sound rung through the eerie woods once again. By now the sun had set behind the clouds and darkness rang through the summer sky.

Aaron knew his mother would send a search party within minutes if he didn't return home but he just had to find out the source of that growling sound.

"WHO IS THAT?" he screamed! His body shaking from fear, he was torn between running away and running towards the sound. He figured the source of the noise had to be close so he decided to take a few steps to see what was making the noise.

As he inched deeper and deeper into the woods, each step found him trembling uncontrollably. The sound was so loud it felt like an earthquake rumbling beneath his feet. Someone must have heard it but the neighborhood was so quite you could hear a pin drop. "How did no one hear that!?".

Pretty soon Aaron was so deep into the words that trees surrounded him in every corner and he could no longer see the playground. He heard the sound once again, much louder and scarier this time. Aaron stopped in his tracks, he knew that whatever it was, it was very close. He turned his head slowly to the left and what he saw next left him paralyzed.

Deep in the belly of the forrest laid an enormous bright red figure. His long neck had spikes at the top with large holes all over it. A pair of wide gigantic wings hovered above the forrest. He had two legs. His stomach rippled like the skin of an alligator and his tail was heavy, thick and seemed to stretch for miles. He was an unbelievable magnificent creature but despite his scary figure, there was sadness in his eyes.

"Are…you….a dragon?" Aaron asked slowly, his voice stuttering with every syllable.

Yes said the red dragon.

Aaron quickly relaxed something about the red dragon seemed gentle and fragile. He wasn't afraid of his enormous frame. In fact, he found it absolutely stunning. Aaron's breathing settled to a normal pace as he inched closer towards the dragon.

"Are you a fire breathing dragon, like the ones in the movies?"

"Yes, wanna see?" Next thing Aaron saw was a huge flame of fire lighting up the sky, it sounded like a huge truck engine rumbling. Aaron's bright brown eyes lit up in delight. Again he wondered how no one heard or saw what was happening.

"Am I the only one that can see you?" he asked curiously.

"Yes" said the dragon.

"How come?" asked Aaron.

"Because you believe." Said the dragon softly. "Aaron, I need your help."

"What's wrong?" asked Aaron concerned, nearing closer to the dragon as he felt more comfortable.

"My right wing is hurt, I hit a tree on my way down and now I can't fly back home."

"Can I see…?" Aaron asked as the dragon lowered his wing so he could inspect it. Aaron brushed his fingers over the bruise slightly noticing a red scar and a deep cut that sunk deep into the dragon's skin.

"I need to heal it so that I can fly back to my family." The dragon said softly.

Aaron was silent while he racked his brain for a quick solution. Then he remembered the first aid kit that was tucked away behind the sand box on the playground. It wasn't too far away and he knew with his speed he would get there in no time.

"Wait here!" he exclaimed. Within seconds he sped off back towards the playground. He leaped over the sand box, grabbed the first aid kit and headed back to the woods to the Dragon.

When Aaron arrived with the first aid kit he said, "It might hurt alittle but trust me."

"I trust you Aaron" said the Dragon softly.

Aaron slowly and gently put the cool antiseptic over the dragon's cut. Within seconds the cut was completely healed.

"Thank you my friend Aaron, because of you I can return to my family. And don't worry you will make it on the team." Aaron exhaled deeply and let out a bright smile. His mind was too flustered to try and figure out how the dragon knew he would make the soccer team.

Then the dragon spread his mighty red wings that seemed to stretch towards the ends of the forrest. His amazing frame rose above the clouds and darted into the sky like the maleficent creature he was. And in his fiery breath he left a message for Aaron across the sky that read, Aaron is my best friend! Aaron stared into the sky with wide eyes and a dropped jaw. It was the most amazing thing he had ever seen.

www.ingramcontent.com/pod-product-compliance
Lightning Source LLC
Chambersburg PA
CBHW041241040426

42445CB00004B/115